Instant GSON

Learn to create JSON data from Java objects and implement
them in an application with the GSON library

Sandeep Kumar Patel

BIRMINGHAM - MUMBAI

Instant GSON

Copyright © 2013 Packt Publishing

First published: August 2013

Production Reference: 1230813

Published by Packt Publishing Ltd.
Livery Place
35 Livery Street
Birmingham B3 2PB, UK.

ISBN 978-1-78328-203-6

www.packtpub.com

Credits

Author

Sandeep Kumar Patel

Reviewers

Shameera Rathnayaka

Karim Varela

Acquisition Editor

Usha Iyer

Commissioning Editor

Amit Ghodake

Technical Editors

Krishnaveni Haridas

Chandni Maishery

Copy Editor

Sayanee Mukherjee

Project Coordinator

Akash Poojary

Proofreader

Julie Jackson

Graphics

Abhinash Sahu

Production Coordinator

Nilesh R. Mohite

Cover Work

Nilesh R. Mohite

Cover Image

Ronak Dhruv

About the Author

Sandeep Kumar Patel is a senior web developer and founder of `www.tutorialsavvy.com`, a widely-read programming blog since 2012. He has more than four years of experience in object-oriented JavaScript and JSON-based web applications development. He is GATE-2005 Information Technology (IT) qualified and has a Masters degree from VIT University, Vellore. At present, he holds the position of senior development engineer in Pramati Technology. You can know more about him from his LinkedIn profile (`http://www.linkedin.com/in/techblogger`).

He has received the Dzone Most Valuable Blogger (MVB) award for technical publications related to web technologies. His article can be viewed at `http://www.dzone.com/users/sandeepgiet`.

He has also received the Java Code Geek (JCG) badge for a technical article published in JCG. His article can be viewed at `http://www.javacodegeeks.com/author/sandeep-kumar-patel/`.

I would like to thank the three most important people in my life. My parents Dilip Kumar Patel and Sanjukta Patel for their love; and my wife Surabhi Patel for her support and the joy that she has brought to my life.

A special thanks to the team at Packt Publishing without whom this book wouldn't have been possible.

About the Reviewers

Shameera Rathnayaka is an Apache Axis2 Committer and a PMC member, and has been actively contributing to several Apache projects for the past few years. He holds a BSc Engineering (Hons) degree in Computer Science and Engineering from the University of Moratuwa, Sri Lanka. He first started his open source contributions with the Apache Axis2 project, where he implemented JDK7 Enum support for Apache Axis2, as well as a stream-based, high-performance solution for JSON<-->XML lossless transformation. A two times Google Summer of Code program participant with the Apache Axis2 and Apache Airavata projects, he is currently working on the project named JSON support and JSON to XML bidirectional conversion for Apache Airavata.

He currently works as a software engineer at WSO2 Inc, an open source enterprise middleware company based in Sri Lanka, where he is a member of the WSO2 Carbon team. His main research interest is Distributed Computing.

Karim Varela, the lead Android engineer at Tinder, has almost 10 years experience in mobile application development. He is currently responsible for building Tinder's Android application from the ground up. He is also leading SocialTagg, a startup whose aim is to connect people at events in a better way.

He was a technical reviewer for the book Pro Android 4 and is studying for his MBA from the University of Florida. He holds a bachelor's degree in Computer Science from the University of California.

www.packtpub.com

Support files, eBooks, discount offers, and more

You might want to visit www.packtpub.com for support files and downloads related to your book.

Did you know that Packt offers eBook versions of every book published, with PDF and e-Pub files available? You can upgrade to the eBook version at www.packtpub.com and as a print book customer, you are entitled to a discount on the eBook copy. Get in touch with us at service@packtpub.com for more details.

At www.packtpub.com, you can also read a collection of free technical articles, sign up for a range of free newsletters, and receive exclusive discounts and offers on Packt books and eBooks.

packtlib.packtpub.com

Do you need instant solutions to your IT questions? PacktLib is Packt's online digital book library. Here, you can access, read, and search across Packt's entire library of books.

Why Subscribe?

- ✦ Fully searchable across every book published by Packt
- ✦ Copy and paste, print, and bookmark content
- ✦ On demand and accessible via web browser

Free Access for Packt account holders

If you have an account with Packt at www.packtpub.com, you can use this to access PacktLib today and view nine entirely free books. Simply use your login credentials for immediate access.

Table of Contents

Instant GSON

Welcome to *Instant GSON*. This book has been especially created to provide you with all the information that you need to get started with GSON. You will learn the basics of GSON, get started with building JSON representation, and discover some tips and tricks for coding GSON.

This book contains the following sections:

So, what is GSON? helps you find out what GSON actually is, what you can do with it, and why it's so great.

Configuring GSON in Eclipse will help you configure the GSON library in Eclipse IDE for a simple Java project and a Maven type Project.

Quick start – creating your first JSON in GSON will show you how to perform one of the core tasks of GSON: creating courses. Follow the examples discussed in this section to get started with GSON, which will be the common code of most of the GSON use.

Top 12 features you need to know about helps you learn how to perform handling generic-typed, custom serialization and field exclusion strategy. By the end of this section you will be able to:

- ✦ Convert a Java object to JSON
- ✦ Serialize and deserialize in GSON
- ✦ Use the GSON nested classes handling mechanism
- ✦ Convert a Java array to a JSON array
- ✦ Handle generic-type classes while working with GSON serialization and deserialization
- ✦ Handle a null object while working with GSON
- ✦ Use versioning support in GSON

- ✦ Use the no argument constructor support
- ✦ Create a custom field name from a Java object to JSON output string
- ✦ Exclude a JSON field while serializing it in GSON

People and places you should get to know provides you with many useful links to the project page and forums, as well as a number of helpful articles, tutorials, blogs, and Twitter feeds by the GSON super-contributors, as every open source project is centered around a community.

So, what is GSON?

In this section, we will cover the JSON data exchange format and its significance, and give an introduction to the GSON library. Finally, we will look up the GSON library and its top features.

This chapter distills the theory of data exchange format from the main core. No previous knowledge about the subject is necessary, but I assume that you are familiar with the fundamentals of JavaScript.

The data exchange format is a very vital area of information technology. Data is read and consumed by many heterogeneous applications to form information. The heterogeneous nature means these applications take the input data in their proprietary format. This requires the input data to be preformatted before it is consumed by the main application, which adds an additional level of complexity to an application. To address this need, a common data exchange format is put in place for communication. This has led to the origin of many popular standard formats such as XML, YAML, and JSON.

Java Script Object Notation (**JSON**) originates from the most rocking JavaScript language. JSON has derived its syntax from JavaScript objects. In JavaScript, an object can be created by using the `new` keyword or anonymously. An anonymous JavaScript object can be created using curly braces with or without a key/value pair.

A typical anonymous JavaScript object syntax is as follows:

```
{}, {key: value}, {key1: value1, key2: value2}…
```

In the JavaScript language, almost everything is treated as an object, starting from a function to an array. A typical anonymous array in JavaScript can follow one of the following syntaxes:

```
[], [{}], [{key: value}], [{key1: value1}, {key2: value2}...
```

Let's test it:

```
VarnumberArray = [10,20,30,40];
console.log (typeofnumberArray);
```

The output of the preceding code is an object.

In the Firebug console, it would look as follows:

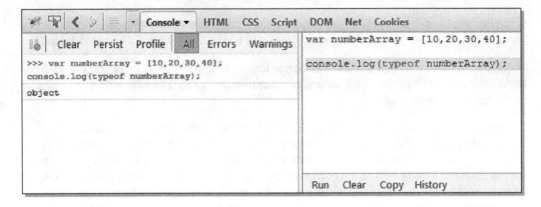

In the preceding code, a JavaScript array is defined with numbers as elements. In the second line, we are printing its type on the console. It displays the **object** text in the **Console**. From the output, it is evident that arrays in JavaScript are objects.

A Web 2.0-based client and server application exchanges data in AJAX mode. XML and JSON are the most preferred data formats in web application development. JSON is the most preferred for the data interchange format because of its following features:

✦ **Lightweight in footprints**: The size of a JSON response or file is much smaller than that of an XML one.

✦ **Native nature**: All browsers have JavaScript as their native language and JSON follows the same object concept of JavaScript, which makes its rendering faster.

✦ **Simpler syntax**: JSON has simpler syntaxes to represent data comprising curly braces and the key/value pairs separated by a colon. This makes the job of parsing easier.

GSON is an open source application programming interface project written in the Java language for handling the JSON data format. It converts a Java object into its JSON representation. It can also be used to convert a JSON string into an equivalent Java object.

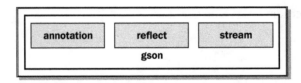

The root `gson` package contains all the common classes and interfaces for JSON data handling. The subpackages inside `gson` are `reflect`, `annotation`, and `stream`. The `reflect` package holds the classes and interfaces that deal with information on the Java generic types. The `annotation` package contains the related classes and interfaces for custom name mapping for object properties. The `stream` package contains the classes and interfaces that are related to reading and writing to and from a stream.

Initial goals of the GSON designs are as follows:

✦ To have a simple conversion mechanism for converting a Java object to and from JSON. The GSON Java project has a large number of utility methods exposed as APIs for the developers to use.

✦ To allow pre-existing unmodifiable Java objects to be converted to and from JSON.

✦ To customize the representation of objects. GSON provides custom mapping of names for the object fields while serializing it to a JSON string.

✦ To provide a compact and formatted output. By default, the generated JSON string for a Java object is in a compact form. GSON provides pretty printing facilities to get it in the human-readable format.

Configuring GSON in Eclipse

In this section, you will learn about configuring the GSON library in Eclipse IDE for a simple Java project and a Maven type project.

Getting the GSON library

The GSON library project is an open source project and is hosted by Google. This project is free for download and its use is based on Apache License 2.0. The current release of this library is 2.2.2.

The base URL of this library is `http://code.google.com/p/google-gson`. Navigate to the download section of this page and download the zipped version (`google-gson-2.2.2-release.zip`). To verify the correct download of this ZIP file, you can compare the checksum that is provided at the base site of GSON.

You can see the following five files when you unzip the downloaded file. Two of them are text files and the other three are JAR files:

File	Type	Details
`License`	Text	This text file has all the description about Apache License 2.0 and its use
`ReadMe`	Text	This text file contains the information and purpose of the GSON library
`gson-2.2.2-sources`	JAR	This JAR file contains all the source code for the GSON library
`gson-2.2.2-javadoc`	JAR	This JAR file contains the entire Java document generated by the GSON project
`gson-2.2.2`	JAR	This JAR file is your required GSON library

Configuring a Java project

To configure the GSON library in Eclipse for a Java project, a developer needs to execute the following steps:

1. Create a new Java project in the Eclipse workspace. For example, GsonDemo.

2. Create a new folder, say lib, inside the GsonDemo Java project and paste the gson-2.2.2.jar file in it.

3. Add the JAR file in CLASSPATH of the project, and GSON is now all set to be used:

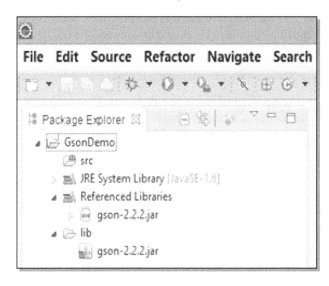

The preceding screenshot shows that the gson library is added to the Java project. Now, the GSON JAR file is listed in the Referenced Libraries.

Configuring a Maven project

All Maven project file dependencies are maintained by a project object model. In Maven 2, this file is known as pom.xml. All project specific configurations are added as dependencies in the plugin section of pom.xml.

There is a standard format to add a dependency to a Maven type of project. It requires certain tags and values to be included. To add the GSON dependency to a Maven-type project, perform the following steps:

1. Create a Maven Java/Web project of JAR/WAR archetype, GsonMavenDemo.

2. Add the GSON dependency in the plugin tag by using the dependency XML tag.

The XML file looks as follows:

```xml
<dependencies>
<dependency>
<groupId>com.google.code.gson</groupId>
<artifactId>gson</artifactId>
<version>2.2.2</version>
<scope>compile</scope>
</dependency>
</dependencies>
```

3. Save the pom.xml file and use the install Maven option. Maven install looks through the Maven repository on the network and downloads the GSON library to the Maven dependency:

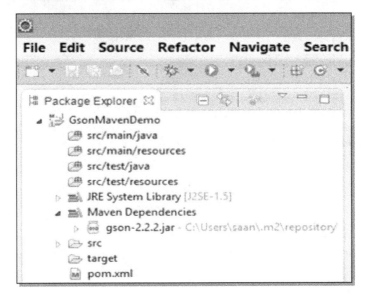

In the preceding screenshot, after the Maven installation, the GSON library JAR file gets added to the Maven Dependencies folder.

Quick start – creating your first JSON in GSON

In this section, you will learn different ways to instantiate GSON and their significance, followed by a quick example code that shows the basic serialization of wrapper type Java objects.

Step 1 – instantiating GSON

To use the GSON library, an object of the `com.google.gson.Gson` class needs to be instantiated. A GSON object does not maintain any state; this characteristic helps in reusing the GSON object at multiple places.

The GSON library provides two ways for instantiating it:

+ The default approach
+ The builder approach with settings

The default approach

In this approach, the GSON class object can be instantiated using the `new` keyword. This approach creates a `gsonobject` instance without any setting.

The builder approach

In this approach, a GSON class object can be created using the `GsonBuilder` class and the `create` method:

```
Gsongson = new GsonBuilder ().create ();
```

The preceding code calls the `create` method of `GsonBuilder`, which returns a `Gson` object for initialization.

There are more methods present for various settings of the `Gson` object, such as pretty printing and setting lenient property, which we will explore in a later section of this book.

The following table shows some of the methods exposed by the GSON object:

Methods	Description
`fromJson`	This method is used for deserialization to get Java objects. There are many overloaded forms of this method, which are available in its API.
`toJson`	This method serializes the Java object into its equivalent JSON representation. There are many overloaded forms of this method, which are available in its API.
`toJsonTree`	This method serializes objects with their generic types. Other overloaded versions are also available for use in its API.

A quick example

Let's see a quick example code that shows the basic use of the GSON library for serializing/ deserializing a Java wrapper-type object to and from the JSON string:

```
importcom.google.gson.Gson;

public class QuickStartDemo {

public static void main(String[] args){

Gsongson = new Gson();

/*Java Wrapper Type*/
String jsonInteger = gson.toJson(new Integer(1));
String jsonDouble = gson.toJson(new Double(12345.5432));

System.out.println("GSON toJson Method Use ");
System.out.println(jsonInteger);
System.out.println(jsonDouble);

Integer javaInteger = gson.fromJson(jsonInteger, Integer.class);
Double javaDouble = gson.fromJson(jsonDouble, Double.class);

System.out.println("GSON fromJson Method Use ");
System.out.println(javaInteger);
System.out.println(javaDouble);
}
}
```

The output of the preceding code is as follows:

GSON toJson Method Use

1

12345.5432

GSON fromJson Method Use

1

12345.5432

The preceding code shows a quick use of the two basic methods `toJson` and `fromJson`.

In the first section of the code, a `Gson` class object is instantiated using the default method, and two Java wrapper-type objects, `Integer` and `Double`, are instantiated with values `1` and `12345.5432`.These objects are passed to the `toJson` method that produces their JSON equivalent strings:

Method	Details
toJSON	✦ **Parameter**: This method takes a Java class-type object for serialization
	✦ **Return**: This method returns a JSON representation of the object in the string format
fromJSON	✦ **Parameter**: The first parameter is of a type of string of the JSON representation, and the second parameter is an intended Java class type
	✦ **Return**: It returns an intended Java class-type object

In the last section of the code, the JSON equivalent strings are passed to the `fromJson` method. This method takes two parameters, the first parameter is a string and the second parameter is an expected Java class type. The return type of the `fromJson` method is always an intended Java type.

Top 12 features you need to know about

In this section, you will learn about the top features supported by the GSON library. You will also learn about how to implement these features.

Java objects support

Objects in GSON are referred as types of **JsonElement**:

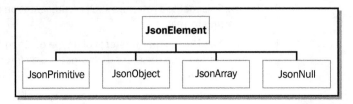

The GSON library can convert any user-defined class objects to and from the JSON representation. The Student class is a user-defined class, and GSON can serialize any Student object to JSON.

The Student.java class is as follows:

```java
public class Student {

private String name;

private String subject;

privateint mark;

public String getName() {
return name;
}

public void setName(String name) {
this.name = name;
}

public String getSubject() {
return subject;
}
```

```
public void setSubject(String subject) {
this.subject = subject;
}

public int getMark() {
return mark;
}

public void setMark(int mark) {
this.mark = mark;
}

}
```

The code for `JavaObjectFeaturesUse.java` is as follows:

```
import com.google.gson.Gson;
importcom.packt.chapter.vo.Student;

public class JavaObjectFeaturesUse {

public static void main(String[] args){

Gsongson = new Gson();

Student aStudent = new Student();
aStudent.setName("Sandeep");
aStudent.setMark(128);
aStudent.setSubject("Computer Science");

String studentJson = gson.toJson(aStudent);
System.out.println(studentJson);

Student anotherStudent = gson.fromJson(studentJson, Student.class);
System.out.println(anotherStudentinstanceof  Student);
  }
}
```

The output of the preceding code is as follows:

{"name":"Sandeep","subject":"Computer Science","mark":128}

True

The preceding code creates a Student object with name as Sandeep, subject as Computer Science, and marks as 128. A Gson object is then instantiated and the Student object is passed in as a parameter to the toJson() method. It returns a string that has the JSON representation of the Java object. This string is printed as the first line in the console. The output JSON representation of the Student object is a collection of key/value pairs. The Java property of the Student class becomes the key in the JSON string.

In the last part of the code, the fromJson() method takes the JSON generated string as the first input parameter and Student.class as the second parameter, to convert the JSON string back to a Student Java object. The last line of the code uses an instance of Student as the second-line operator to verify whether the generated Java object by the fromJson() method is of type Student. In the console, it prints **True** as the output, and if we print the values, we will get the same values as in JSON.

Serialization and deserialization

GSON has implicit serializations for some classes, such as Java wrapper type (Integer, Long, Double, and so on), java.net.URL, java.net.URI, java.util.Date, and so on.

Let's see an example:

```java
import java.util.Date;
import com.google.gson.Gson;

public class InbuiltSerializerFeature {

public static void main(String[] args) {

Date aDateJson = new Date();
Gsongson = new Gson();
String jsonDate = gson.toJson(aDateJson);

System.out.println(jsonDate);
}

}
```

The output of the preceding code is as follows:

May 29, 2013 8:55:07 PM

The preceding code is serializing the Java `Date` class object to its JSON representation. In the preceding section, you have learned how GSON is used to serialize and deserialize objects, and how it supports custom serializers and deserializers for user-defined Java class objects. Let's see how it works.

Also, GSON provides the custom serialization feature to developers.

The following code is an example of a custom serializer:

```
classStudentTypeSerializer implements JsonSerializer<Student>{

@Override
publicJsonElement serialize(Student student, Type type,
JsonSerializationContextcontext) {

JsonObjectobj = new JsonObject();

obj.addProperty("studentname", student.getName());

obj.addProperty("subjecttaken", student.getSubject());

obj.addProperty("marksecured", student.getMark());

returnobj;
}
}
```

The following code is an example of a custom deserializer:

```
classStudentTypeDeserializer implements JsonDeserializer<Student>{

@Override
public Student deserialize(JsonElementjsonelment, Type type,
JsonDeserializationContext context) throws JsonParseException {

JsonObjectjsonObject = jsonelment.getAsJsonObject();

Student aStudent = new Student();
```

```
aStudent.setName(jsonObject.get("studentname").getAsString());

aStudent.setSubject(jsonObject.get("subjecttaken").getAsString());

aStudent.setMark(jsonObject.get("marksecured").getAsInt());

return aStudent;
}

}
```

The following code tests the custom serializer and deserializer:

```
import java.lang.reflect.Type;
import com.google.gson.Gson;
importcom.google.gson.GsonBuilder;
importcom.google.gson.JsonDeserializationContext;
importcom.google.gson.JsonDeserializer;
importcom.google.gson.JsonElement;
importcom.google.gson.JsonObject;
importcom.google.gson.JsonParseException;
importcom.google.gson.JsonSerializationContext;
importcom.google.gson.JsonSerializer;
public class CustomSerializerFeature {

public static void main(String[] args) {

GsonBuildergsonBuilder = new GsonBuilder();

gsonBuilder.registerTypeAdapter(Student.class, new
StudentTypeSerializer());


Gsongson = gsonBuilder.create();

  Student aStudent = new Student();

aStudent.setName("Sandeep");

aStudent.setMark(150);

aStudent.setSubject("Arithmetic");

  String studentJson = gson.toJson(aStudent);
```

```
System.out.println("Custom Serializer : Json String Representation ");
System.out.println(studentJson);

 Student anotherStudent = gson.fromJson(studentJson, Student.class);

System.out.println("Custom DeSerializer : Java Object Creation");
System.out.println("Student Name "+anotherStudent.getName());
System.out.println("Student Mark "+anotherStudent.getMark());
System.out.println("Student Subject "+anotherStudent.getSubject());
System.out.println("is anotherStudent is type of Student
"+(anotherStudentinstanceof Student));
}
}
```

The output of the preceding code is as follows:

Custom Serializer : Json String Representation

{"studentname":"Sandeep","subjecttaken":"Arithmetic","marksecured":150}

Custom DeSerializer : Java Object Creation

Student Name Sandeep

Student Mark 150

Student Subject Arithmetic

is anotherStudent is type of Student true

Pretty printing

The JSON representation of the serialized output of GSON is in compact format. If there is a huge collection of Java objects and each object has many properties that are serialized, their compact JSON representation is unreadable and looks ugly.

To address this issue, `GsonBuilder` supports pretty printing configuration, while creating a `Gson` object for serialization use. This pretty printing feature beautifies the JSON string output with proper tab indentation and new line breaks.

The following are some important points on the formatter:

✦ `JsonPrintFormatter` and `JsonCompactFormatter` are two formatter types present in GSON.

✦ `JsonCompactFormatter` is the default formatter for GSON.

◆ JsonPrintFormatter is used for pretty printing and it is not exposed in the API. So it cannot be changed by the developer.

◆ JsonPrintFormatter supports a default line length of 80 characters, two character indentations, and four character right margins.

◆ JsonPrintFormatter can be used by calling a setPrettyPrinting() method on GsonBuilder.

Let's see an example of pretty printing:

```java
import java.util.ArrayList;
import java.util.List;
import com.google.gson.Gson;
import com.google.gson.GsonBuilder;
import com.packt.chapter.vo.Student;

 public class PrettyPrintFeature {


  public static void main(String[] args) {

    Gson gson = new GsonBuilder().setPrettyPrinting().create();
    List<Student> listOfStudent = new ArrayList<Student>();

    Student student1 = new Student();
    student1.setName("Sandeep Kumar Patel");
    student1.setSubject("Arithmetic");
    student1.setMark(234);

    Student student2 = new Student();
    student2.setName("Sangeeta Patel");
    student2.setSubject("Geography");
    student2.setMark(214);

    listOfStudent.add(student1);
    listOfStudent.add(student2);

    String prettyJsonString = gson.toJson(listOfStudent);
    System.out.println(prettyJsonString);
  }


}
```

The output of the previous code is as follows:

```
[
  {
    "name": "Sandeep Kumar Patel",
    "subject": "Arithmetic",
    "mark": 234
  },
  {
    "name": "Sangeeta Patel",
    "subject": "Geography",
    "mark": 214
  }
]
```

The previous code serializes a list of students to the JSON representation. It uses the `GsonBuilder` class for getting a `Gson` object. The `setPrettyPrinting()` method is used to configure pretty printing .You can see that the output of the previous code is properly indented and tabbed, and is pleasant to read.

Nested classes

A Java nested class can be of two types:

+ Static nested class
+ Pure nested class (instance inner class)

In this section we will see how GSON handles each of these types of nested class objects.

Static nested class

GSON can serialize/deserialize a static nested class implicitly. No additional configuration is required.

Let's see an example of a static nested class:

```
import com.google.gson.Gson;
import com.google.gson.GsonBuilder;

class Student{

  private String studentName;

  private int mark;

  public String getStudentName() {
    return studentName;
  }
```

```
    public void setStudentName(String studentName) {
      this.studentName = studentName;
    }

    public int getMark() {
      return mark;
    }

    public void setMark(int mark) {
      this.mark = mark;
    }

    public static class Course{

      private String courseName;

      private String duration;

      public String getCourseName() {
        return courseName;
      }

      public void setCourseName(String courseName) {
        this.courseName = courseName;
      }

      public String getDuration() {
        return duration;
      }

      public void setDuration(String duration) {
        this.duration = duration;
      }
    }
  }
public class StaticNestedClassFeature {

  public static void main(String[] args) {

    Gson gson = new GsonBuilder().setPrettyPrinting().create();

    Student.Course aCourse = new Student.Course();
    aCourse.setCourseName("M.TECH.");
    aCourse.setDuration("120 hr");
```

```
String jsonCourse = gson.toJson(aCourse);
System.out.println(jsonCourse);

Student.Course anotherCourse = gson.fromJson(jsonCourse,
    Student.Course.class);

System.out.println("Course :
    "+anotherCourse.getCourseName()+"Duration :
    "+anotherCourse.getDuration());
    }
}
```

The output of the previous code is as follows:

```
{
   "courseName": "M.TECH.",
   "duration": "120 hr"
}
Course : M.TECH.Duration : 120 hr
```

In the previous code, `Course` is a static nested class inside the `Student` class. `courseName` and `duration` are two properties, and their respective `getter` and `setter` methods are present in it. A static inner class can be instantiated in Java by calling the outer class with a `dot` operator. The line `Student.Course aCourse = new Student.Course()` is for initializing the nested class course. `M.TECH.` and `120 hr` are two values used to instantiate it. From the output, it is evident that GSON is able to serialize the static nested class that produces the JSON representation of the `Course` object. The last line of the output shows that GSON has successfully deserialized it.

Pure nested class

A pure nested class in Java can be instantiated by using the outer class object. The following code demonstrates how GSON can serialize and deserialize a pure nested Java class object:

```
import com.google.gson.Gson;
import com.google.gson.GsonBuilder;

class Student{

  private String studentName;
  private int mark;

  public String getStudentName() {
    return studentName;
  }
```

```
      public void setStudentName(String studentName) {
        this.studentName = studentName;
      }
      public int getMark() {
        return mark;
      }
      public void setMark(int mark) {
        this.mark = mark;
      }
      public  class Course{

        private String courseName;

        private String duration;

        public String getCourseName() {
          return courseName;
        }
        public void setCourseName(String courseName) {
          this.courseName = courseName;
        }
        public String getDuration() {
          return duration;
        }
        public void setDuration(String duration) {
          this.duration = duration;
        }
      }
    }

public class InstanceNestedClassFeature {

  public static void main(String[] args) {

    Gson gson = new GsonBuilder().setPrettyPrinting().create();
    Student outstudent = new Student();
    Student.Course instanceCourse = outstudent.new Course();

     instanceCourse.setCourseName("M.TECH.");
    instanceCourse.setDuration("12 hr");

    String jsonCourse = gson.toJson(instanceCourse);
    System.out.println(jsonCourse);

    Student.Course anotherCourse = gson.fromJson(jsonCourse,
      Student.Course.class);
```

```
    System.out.println("Course :
      "+anotherCourse.getCourseName()+"Duration :
      "+anotherCourse.getDuration());
  }
}
```

The output of the previous code is as follows:

```
{
  "courseName": "M.TECH.",
  "duration": "12 hr"
}
Course : M.TECH.Duration : 12 hr
```

In the previous code, Course is a pure inner class with two fields and their getter and setter methods. A Course class object's instanceCourse is instantiated using the outer class object outstudent. This inner class object is put to serialization and deserialization, which produces the result on the console. During deserialization, the fromJson() method takes the second parameter as Student.Course, which helps GSON to successfully deserialize it to a nested class object.

Array

GSON supports the conversion of Java arrays to and from the JSON representation.

Let's see an example of arrays:

```
import com.google.gson.Gson;
import com.google.gson.GsonBuilder;

public class ArrayFeature {

  public static void main(String[] args) {

    Gson gson = new GsonBuilder().create();

    int[] numberArray = {121, 23, 34, 44, 52};

    String[] fruitsArray = {"apple", "oranges", "grapes"};

    String jsonNumber = gson.toJson(numberArray);
    String jsonString = gson.toJson(fruitsArray);

    System.out.println(jsonNumber);
    System.out.println(jsonString);
```

```
    int [] numCollectionArray = gson.fromJson(jsonNumber,
      int[].class);
    String[] fruitBasketArray = gson.fromJson(jsonString,
      String[].class);

    System.out.println("Number Array Length
      "+numCollectionArray.length);
    System.out.println("Fruit Array Length
      "+fruitBasketArray.length);

  }

}
```

The output of the previous code is as follows:

```
[121,23,34,44,52]
["apple","oranges","grapes"]
Number Array Length 5
Fruit Array Length 3
```

The previous code shows two arrays, `numberArray` and `fruitsArray`, of type `integer` and `string` respectively. They are serialized and deserialized sequentially.

Generic type

GSON supports generic-type Java class objects for serialization and deserialization using the `com.google.gson.reflect.TypeToken` class. The purpose of using the `TypeToken` class is to use the `Type Erasure` feature of Java generic types.

`Type Erasure` is the phase that occurs during compile time, where Java generic types are removed completely to produce byte code. So while deserializing a JSON string to a generic Java class, it may not be deserialized correctly.

The following code demonstrates the generic type serialization/deserialization and how the `TypeToken` class is used to address this issue:

```
import java.lang.reflect.Type;
import com.google.gson.Gson;
import com.google.gson.reflect.TypeToken;

class StudentGeneric<T, E> {

  T mark;

  E name;
```

```java
  public T getMark() {
    return mark;
  }

  public void setMark(T mark) {
    this.mark = mark;
  }

  public E getName() {
    return name;
  }

  public void setName(E name) {
    this.name = name;
  }
}

public class GenericTypeFeature {

  @SuppressWarnings("unchecked")
  public static void main(String[] args) {

    Gson gson = new Gson();
    StudentGeneric<Integer, String> studGenericObj1 = new
      StudentGeneric<Integer, String>();
    studGenericObj1.setMark(25);
    studGenericObj1.setName("Sandeep");

    String json = gson.toJson(studGenericObj1);
    System.out.println("Serialized Output :");
    System.out.println(json);

    StudentGeneric<Integer, String> studGenericObj2 =
      gson.fromJson(json,
    StudentGeneric.class);
    System.out.println("DeSerialized Output :");
    System.out.println("Mark : " + studGenericObj2.getMark());

    Type studentGenericType = new
      TypeToken<StudentGeneric<Integer, String>>() {
    }.getType();
    StudentGeneric<Integer, String> studGenericObj3 =
      gson.fromJson(json,
    studentGenericType);
    System.out.println("TypeToken Use DeSerialized Output :");
    System.out.println("Mark : " + studGenericObj3.getMark());
  }

}
```

The output of the previous code is as follows:

```
Serialized Output :
{"mark":25,"name":"Sandeep"}
DeSerialized Output :
Mark : 25.0
TypeToken Use DeSerialized Output :
Mark : 25
```

In the previous code, a `StudentGeneric` class takes two generic parameters and has their respective `getter` and `setter` methods. A `StudentGeneric` class object is created using `integer` and `string` as types for `mark` and `name`. While serializing a student, `mark` is initialized to `25`, but the deserialized output shows it as `25.0`, which is an incorrect value, as the `Type Erasure` property removes the generic-type parameters from the class at compile time. The `TypeToken` class is used to resolve this problem. The `getType()` method returns the original class type with generic parameters, which helps GSON to correctly deserialize the object and output the correct value as `25`.

Null object support

GSON is also capable of serializing/deserializing null Java objects to and from the JSON representation.

Let's see an example of null objects:

```java
import com.google.gson.Gson;
import com.google.gson.GsonBuilder;
public class NullSupportFeature {

  public static void main(String[] args) {
    Gson gson = new
      GsonBuilder().serializeNulls()
      .setPrettyPrinting().create();

    Student aStudent = new Student();
    aStudent.setName("Sandeep Kumar Patel");
    aStudent.setSubject(null);
   aStudent.setMark(234);

    String studentJson = gson.toJson(aStudent);

    System.out.println(studentJson);

    Student javaStudentObject = gson.fromJson(studentJson,
      Student.class);
```

```
      System.out.println("Student Subject
        "+javaStudentObject.getSubject());
      System.out.println("Student Name
        "+javaStudentObject.getName());
    }

  }
```

The output of the previous code is as follows:

```
{
   "name": "Sandeep Kumar Patel",
   "subject": null,
   "mark": 234,
   "gender": null
}
Student Subject   null
Student Name   Sandeep Kumar Patel
```

Versioning support

GSON provides the versioned serialization/deserialization of Java objects to and from the JSON representation. This helps in iterative development and release of value objects. The GSON API provides a mechanism to cater to these requests for different versions of data.

Let's see an example of versioning:

```
import com.google.gson.Gson;
import com.google.gson.GsonBuilder;
import com.google.gson.annotations.Since;

@Since(1.0)
class Student {

  private String name;

  private String subject;

  private int mark;

  @Since(1.1) private String gender;

  public String getGender() {
    return gender;
  }
```

```java
    public void setGender(String gender) {
      this.gender = gender;
    }

    public String getName() {
      return name;
    }

    public void setName(String name) {
      this.name = name;
    }

    public String getSubject() {
      return subject;
    }

    public void setSubject(String subject) {
      this.subject = subject;
    }

    public int getMark() {
      return mark;
    }

    public void setMark(int mark) {
      this.mark = mark;
    }

}

public class VersionSupportFeature {

  public static void main(String[] args) {

    Student aStudent = new Student();
    aStudent.setName("Sandeep Kumar Patel");
    aStudent.setSubject("Algebra");
    aStudent.setMark(534);
    aStudent.setGender("Male");

    System.out.println("Student json for Version 1.0 ");
    Gson gson = new
      GsonBuilder().setVersion(1.0).setPrettyPrinting().create();
    String jsonOutput = gson.toJson(aStudent);
    System.out.println(jsonOutput);
```

```
      System.out.println("Student json for Version 1.1 ");
      gson = new
        GsonBuilder().setVersion(1.1).setPrettyPrinting().create();
      jsonOutput = gson.toJson(aStudent);
      System.out.println(jsonOutput);
    }
  }
```

The output of the previous code is as follows:

```
Student json for Version 1.0
{
  "name": "Sandeep Kumar Patel",
  "subject": "Algebra",
  "mark": 534
}
Student json for Version 1.1
{
  "name": "Sandeep Kumar Patel",
  "subject": "Algebra",
  "mark": 534,
  "gender": "Male"
}
```

No argument constructor support

While serializing/deserializing a Java object to and from `JSONstring`, GSON creates a default instance of that class using its default constructor. It is good to have a default no argument constructor of the Java class. If a class does not have a default constructor, GSON provides a `class.google.gson.InstanceCreator` interface implementation to deal with it.

Method	Detail
createInstance	Parameter: Takes a parameter of type `java.lang.reflect.Type` Return: A default object instance of type T. T refers to the type of class asked for object instance

Let's see an example of a no argument constructor:

```
import java.lang.reflect.Type;
import com.google.gson.Gson;
import com.google.gson.GsonBuilder;
import com.google.gson.InstanceCreator;
```

```
class Employee {

  private String name;
  private Salary salary;

  public String getName() {
    return name;
  }
  public void setName(String name) {
    this.name = name;
  }
  public Salary getSalary() {
    return salary;
  }
  public void setSalary(Salary salary) {
    this.salary = salary;
  }
  @Override
  public String toString() {
    return "Employee [name=" + name + ", salary=" + salary + " ]";
  }
}

class Salary {

  private int salaryAmount;
  Salary(int salary) {
    this.salaryAmount = salary;
  }
  @Override
  public String toString() {
    return "Salary [salaryAmount=" + salaryAmount + "]";
  }
}

class SalaryInstanceCreator implements InstanceCreator<Salary> {
  @Override
  public Salary createInstance(Type type) {
    return new Salary(25000);
  }
}

public class InstanceCreatorUse {

  public static void main(String[] args) {
```

```
String jsonString = "{\"name\" :\"Sandeep\" , \"salary\": {}}";

Gson gson = new GsonBuilder().serializeNulls()
.registerTypeAdapter(Salary.class, new SalaryInstanceCreator())
.setPrettyPrinting().create();

System.out.println(gson.fromJson(jsonString, Employee.class));
    }
}
```

The previous code demonstrates a JSON string of type `Employee`, which is deserialized to the `Employee`-type class object.

+ **Input**: A JSON string

  ```
  jsonString = "{\"name\" :\"Sandeep\" , \"salary\": {}}";
  ```

+ **Output**: A Java object, a `toString()` method printed in console

  ```
  Employee [name=Sandeep, salary=Salary [salaryAmount=25000]]
  ```

A class `SalaryInstanceCreator` is implemented using `com.google.gson.InstanceCreator` and overrides the `createInstance()` method, which returns a parameterized `Salary` constructor of value `25000`.

This `SalaryInstanceCreator` is registered to GSON as `registerTypeAdapter()`.

When GSON finds the empty `salary` string, it looks for the default constructor of type `Salary`. As default `Salary` constructor is not present, it looks for `GsonBuilder` settings for a type adapter and finds `SalaryInstanceCreator`. It invokes the `createInstance()` method.

So, while deserializing for an empty `Salary` class object, GSON receives `25000` as the default value.

Field naming support

This feature provides flexibility for the developer to give custom names while serializing Java objects. The JSON representation becomes more meaningful and readable.

GSON provides a `FieldNamingPolicy` class with some built-in field naming support:

```
import com.google.gson.FieldNamingPolicy;
import com.google.gson.Gson;
import com.google.gson.GsonBuilder;
import com.google.gson.annotations.SerializedName;


class College{
```

```java
  @SerializedName("instituteName")
  private String name;

  private String[] coursesOffer;

  public String getName() {
    return name;
  }

  public void setName(String name) {
    this.name = name;
  }

  public String[] getCoursesOffer() {
    return coursesOffer;
  }

  public void setCoursesOffer(String[] coursesOffer) {
    this.coursesOffer = coursesOffer;
  }
}

public class FieldNamingFeature {

  public static void main(String[] args) {

  Gson gson = new GsonBuilder().
    setFieldNamingPolicy(FieldNamingPolicy.UPPER_CAMEL_CASE).
    setPrettyPrinting().create();

  College aCollege = new College();
  aCollege.setName("VIT University, Vellore");
  String[] courses = {"BTECH, MTECH, BSC, MSC"};
  aCollege.setCoursesOffer(courses);

  String jsonCollege = gson.toJson(aCollege);
  System.out.println(jsonCollege);
  College anotherCollege = gson.fromJson(jsonCollege,
    College.class);
  System.out.println("College Name : "+anotherCollege.getName);
  }
}
```

The output of the previous code is as follows:

```
{
  "instituteName": "VIT University, Vellore",
  "CoursesOffer": [
    "BTECH, MTECH, BSC, MSC"
  ]
}
College Name : VIT University, Vellore
```

User-defined field naming

Beyond the basic field naming feature, GSON also provides a `FieldNamingStrategy` class to enable developers to create their own field naming policy. The following steps demonstrate how to create a custom field naming policy:

1. Create a Java class implementing the `FieldNamingStrategy` interface.

2. Override the `translateName()` method.

3. This method provides the real implementation of a custom field naming strategy. GSON uses the logic inside this method for a field name while processing a custom field name strategy:

Method	Detail
translateName	Parameter: Takes input parameter of type `java.lang.reflect.Field` Returns: Returns the changed field name as `string`

Let's see an example of user-defined field naming:

```
import java.lang.reflect.Field;
import com.google.gson.FieldNamingStrategy;
import com.google.gson.Gson;
import com.google.gson.GsonBuilder;

class College {

  private String name;

  private String[] coursesOffer;

  public String getName() {
    return name;
  }
}
```

```java
    public void setName(String name) {
      this.name = name;
    }

    public String[] getCoursesOffer() {
      return coursesOffer;
    }

    public void setCoursesOffer(String[] coursesOffer) {
      this.coursesOffer = coursesOffer;
    }
}

class CustomFieldStrategy implements FieldNamingStrategy {

  @Override
  public String translateName(Field aField) {

    String nameOfField = aField.getName();

    return nameOfField.toUpperCase();
  }
}

public class CustomFieldNamingFeature {

  public static void main(String[] args) {

    Gson gson = new GsonBuilder()
    .setFieldNamingStrategy(new CustomFieldStrategy())
    .setPrettyPrinting().create();

    College aCollege = new College();
    aCollege.setName("VIT University, Vellore");
    String[] courses = { "BTECH, MTECH, BSC, MSC" };
    aCollege.setCoursesOffer(courses);

    String jsonCollege = gson.toJson(aCollege);
    System.out.println(jsonCollege);
  }
}
```

The output of the previous code is as follows:

```
{
  "NAME": "VIT University, Vellore",
  "COURSESOFFER": [
    "BTECH, MTECH, BSC, MSC"
  ]
}
```

Field exclusion strategies

GSON API also supports field exclusion during serialization. Developers can exclude some fields while serializing Java objects. GSON provides two different approaches to achieve field exclusion:

+ Configuring GsonBuilder
+ Using Annotation

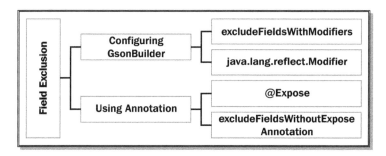

The previous figure shows the abstract of two different approaches for field exclusion strategies in GSON. Each of these approaches is explained in detail.

Configuring GsonBuilder

GsonBuilder provides the `excludeFieldsWithModifiers()` method to exclude fields while serializing. This method provides the capability of excluding all class fields that have the specified modifiers .The prototype signature of this method is as follows:

```
public GsonBuilder excludeFieldsWithModifiers(int... modifiers)
```

+ **Input Parameter**: The ellipsis (...) symbol indicates that it can take any number of parameters of type `java.lang.reflect.Modifier` such as `Modifier.STATIC`, `Modifier.PUBLIC`, and `Modifier.PRIVATE`
+ **Return Type**: It returns a reference object of type `GsonBuilder`

Let's see an example of configuring GsonBuilder:

```java
import java.lang.reflect.Modifier;
import com.google.gson.Gson;
import com.google.gson.GsonBuilder;

class Employee {

  private String name;
  private transient String gender;
  private static String designation;
  protected String department;

  public Employee() {
    this("Abcd Employee", "MALE", "Tech Lead", "IT Services");
  }

  @SuppressWarnings("static-access")
  public Employee(String name, String gender, String
    designation,
  String department) {
    this.name = name;
    this.gender = gender;
    this.designation = designation;
    this.department = department;
  }
}

  public class FieldExclusionFeature {

    public static void main(String[] args) {

      Gson gson = new Gson();

      String json = gson.toJson(new Employee("Sandeep", "Male",
        "Tech Lead","IT Services"));
      System.out.println(json);

      Gson gson2 = new
        GsonBuilder().excludeFieldsWithModifiers().create();
      json = gson2.toJson(new Employee("Sandeep", "MALE", "Tech
        Lead","IT Services"));
      System.out.println(json);
```

```
    Gson gson3 = new GsonBuilder().excludeFieldsWithModifiers(
      Modifier.STATIC).create();
    json = gson3.toJson(new Employee("Sandeep", "MALE", "Tech
      Lead","IT Services"));
    System.out.println(json);
  }


  }
```

The output of the previous code is as follows:

```
{
    "name": "Sandeep",
    "department": "IT Services"
} {
    "name": "Sandeep",
    "gender": "MALE",
    "designation": "TechLead",
    "department": "IT Services"
} {
    "name": "Sandeep",
    "gender": "MALE",
    "department": "IT Services"
}
```

We can derive three points from the previous code:

✦ The first line of the output has an `Employee` JSON string with two fields: `name` and `department`. This output is due to the `Gson` object, which is created using the default approach. For this reason, it omits static and transient fields while serializing.

✦ The second line of the output has an `Employee` JSON string with four fields: `name`, `gender`, `designation`, and `department`. This output is due to the `Gson` object, which is created using the builder approach and `excludeFieldWithModifiers()` method. As no parameters are passed, it serializes all the type of fields present in the `Employee` object.

✦ The third line of the output has an `Employee` JSON string with three fields: `name`, `gender`, and `department`. The output is due to the `Gson` object, which is created using the builder approach, and `excludeFieldsWithModifiers()` method. As `Modifier.STATIC` is passed as a parameter to this method, it does not serialize any static field of the `Employee` object.

Using annotation

GSON provides @Expose annotation to achieve field exclusion during serialization. The field marked with @Expose notation will be serialized to the JSON representation. The GSON excludeFieldsWithoutExposeAnnotation() method must be called while configuring GsonBuilder to use @Expose annotation.

Let's see an example of using @Expose annotation:

```
import com.google.gson.Gson;
import com.google.gson.GsonBuilder;
import com.google.gson.annotations.Expose;

class Vegetable {

  private String name;
  @Expose
  private int price;

  public String getName() {
    return name;
  }

  public void setName(String name) {
    this.name = name;
  }

  public int getPrice() {
    return price;
  }

  public void setPrice(int price) {
    this.price = price;
  }
}

public class FieldExclusionAnnotationUse {

  public static void main(String[] args) {

    Gson gson = new
      GsonBuilder().excludeFieldsWithoutExposeAnnotation()
    .create();
    Vegetable aVegetable = new Vegetable();
    aVegetable.setName("Potato");
    aVegetable.setPrice(26);
    String jsonVegetable = gson.toJson(aVegetable);

    System.out.println("JSON Representation of Vegetable : ");
    System.out.println(jsonVegetable);
  }
}
```

The output of the previous code is as follows:

```
JSON Representation of Vegetable :
{"price":26}
```

We can derive the following points from the previous code:

✦ The output of the previous code has a JSON string with a field `price`. This output is due to the `Gson` object created using the builder approach and `excludeFieldsWithoutExposeAnnotation()` method.

✦ While serializing Java objects, it serializes only the fields with `@Expose` annotation.

User-defined field exclusion annotation

GSON provides flexibility for developers to create a custom annotation for use in the exclusion of fields and classes. The following steps demonstrate how to create a custom annotation:

1. Declaring a marker Java interface. A marker interface is simple a Java interface without any fields or methods. In short, an empty Java interface is a marker interface. The name of this interface will be used as a custom exclusion annotation.

2. A Java class to implement `com.google.gson.ExclusionStrategy`. The `ExclusionStrategy` interface provides two methods. By implementing this interface, the Java class provides the functionality for custom exclusion annotation. When GSON is serializing or deserializing and finds a custom annotation, it looks at the Java class that implemented the `ExclusionStrategy` interface to find out what to do with it.

The `ExclusionStrategy` interface provides two methods:

Method	Details
`shouldSkipField`	Parameter: Takes `FieldAttributes` reference type
	Returns a Boolean value:
	✦ **True**: Field will be a part of serialization/ deserialization output
	✦ **False**: Field will not be a part of serialization/ deserialization output
`shouldSkipClass`	Parameter: Takes `Class` reference type
	Returns a Boolean value:
	✦ **True**: Class will be a part of serialization/ deserialization output
	✦ **False**: Class will not be a part of serialization/ deserialization output

Let's see an example of a user-defined field exclusion annotation:

```
import java.lang.annotation.ElementType;
import java.lang.annotation.Retention;
import java.lang.annotation.RetentionPolicy;
import java.lang.annotation.Target;
import com.google.gson.ExclusionStrategy;
import com.google.gson.FieldAttributes;
import com.google.gson.Gson;
import com.google.gson.GsonBuilder;

@Retention(RetentionPolicy.RUNTIME)
@Target({ ElementType.FIELD })
@interface MyExclude {
}

class CustomExclusionStrategy implements ExclusionStrategy {

  private final Class<?> typeToExclude;

  CustomExclusionStrategy(Class<?> typeToExclude) {
    this.typeToExclude = typeToExclude;
  }

  public boolean shouldSkipClass(Class<?> classname) {
    return (classname == typeToExclude);
  }

  public boolean shouldSkipField(FieldAttributes f) {
    return f.getAnnotation(MyExclude.class) != null;
  }

}

class Vegetable {

  private String name;
  @MyExclude
  private int price;

  public Vegetable() {
  }

  public String getName() {
    return name;
  }
```

```
  public void setName(String name) {
    this.name = name;
  }

  public int getPrice() {
    return price;
  }

  public void setPrice(int price) {
    this.price = price;
  }
}

public class UserDefinedFieldExclusion {

  public static void main(String[] args) {

    Gson gson = new GsonBuilder().setExclusionStrategies(
      new CustomExclusionStrategy(MyExclude.class)).create();

    Vegetable aVegetable = new Vegetable();
    aVegetable.setName("Potato");
    aVegetable.setPrice(26);
    String jsonVegetable = gson.toJson(aVegetable);

    System.out.println(jsonVegetable);
  }
}
```

The output of the previous code is as follows:

```
{"name":"Potato"}
```

The previous code performs the following steps:

1. A user-defined marker annotation @MyExclude is created using the java.lang. annotation package.

2. A new custom exclusion strategy is created by instantiating the CustomExclusionStrategy class with the MyExclude.class parameter.

3. Using the setExclusionStrategies() method, GsonBuilder is configured with this new exclusion strategy.

4. Now the Gson object created from GsonBuilder will exclude fields with @MyExclude annotation.

Applications of GSON

After the invention of the JSON format and its companion language library GSON, the development of Java web applications where a client communicates with a server and responds with data in the JSON format, gained a lot of popularity. This made the Web 2.0 applications successful.

The following `StudentJsonDataServlet.java` shows how a JSON data of type `Student` is returned by a Java servlet and rendered as an HTML table in a browser:

```java
import java.io.IOException;
import java.util.ArrayList;
import java.util.List;
import javax.servlet.ServletException;
import javax.servlet.annotation.WebServlet;
import javax.servlet.http.HttpServlet;
import javax.servlet.http.HttpServletRequest;
import javax.servlet.http.HttpServletResponse;
import com.google.gson.Gson;
import com.packt.myapp.data.Student;

@WebServlet("/StudentJsonDataServlet")
public class StudentJsonDataServlet extends HttpServlet {

    private static final long serialVersionUID = 1L;

    public StudentJsonDataServlet() {}

    protected void doGet(HttpServletRequest request,
        HttpServletResponse response) throws ServletException,
        IOException {

        Gson gson = new Gson();

        List<Student> listOfStudent = getStudentData();

        String jsonString = gson.toJson(listOfStudent);

        response.setContentType("application/json");

        response.getWriter().write(jsonString);
    }

    /**
     * Returns List of Static Student data
     */
    private List<Student> getStudentData(){
```

```
    Student s1 = new Student();
    s1.setName("Sandeep");
    s1.setSubject("Computer");
    s1.setMark(85);

    Student s2 = new Student();
    s2.setName("John");
    s2.setSubject("Science");
    s2.setMark(85);

    Student s3 = new Student();
    s3.setName("Ram");
    s3.setSubject("Computer");
    s3.setMark(85);

    List<Student> listOfStudent = new ArrayList<Student>();
    listOfStudent.add(s1);
    listOfStudent.add(s2);
    listOfStudent.add(s3);

    return listOfStudent;
  }

}
```

The `StudentJsonDataServlet` returns a list of student's details as a JSON string. To indicate to the browser, the data response is a JSON-type header that needs to be set to `application/json`.

The following `studentstableview.html` is the file for rendering the response of the servlet in the browser:

```
<html>
  <head>
  <title>Students JSON Table View</title>
  <script
    src="http://ajax.googleapis.com/ajax/libs/jquery/1.9.1/
    jquery.min.js"></script>
  </head>
  <body>
    <div id="student-data-container"></div>
    <script>
    $(document).ready(function(){

      var getStudentTableHtml, html,
```

```
        htmlStudent, container =$('#student-data-container'),

        ajaxRequest = $.ajax({
          url: "StudentJsonDataServlet",

          dataType: "JSON",

          success: function(data){

            htmlStudent = getStudentTableHtml(data);

            container.html(htmlStudent)
          }
      }),

    getStudentTableHtml = function(data){

      html = [];

      html.push("<TABLE border='2px' cellspacing='2px'>");
      html.push("<TR>");
      html.push("<TH>NAME</TH>");
      html.push("<TH>SUBJECT</TH>");
      html.push("<TH>MARK</TH>");
      html.push("</TR>");

      $.each(data,function(index, aStudent){
        html.push("<TR>");
        html.push("<TD>");
        html.push(aStudent.name);
        html.push("</TD>");
        html.push("<TD>");
        html.push(aStudent.subject);
        html.push("</TD>");
        html.push("<TD>");
        html.push(aStudent.mark);
        html.push("</TD>");
        html.push("</TR>");
      });
      html.push("</TABLE>")

      return html.join("");
    }
  })
    </script>
  </body>
</html>
```

The previous code shows that a jQuery Ajax event is called on a DOM ready event. The servlet uses the GSON API to convert a list of Java `student` objects to its equivalent JSON representation and sends it as a response content. The Firebug console in the following screenshot shows the Ajax request and response in a JSON object:

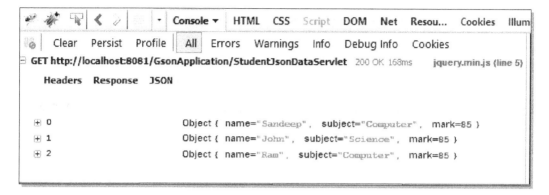

On getting the response, jQuery calls the success handler. In return, the success handler calls the `getStudentTableHtml()` method to build a table in HTML.

This method uses a `for` loop to iterate each `student` JSON object to build the rows of the table. The following screenshot shows an HTML table for students' details built from the `student` JSON response data:

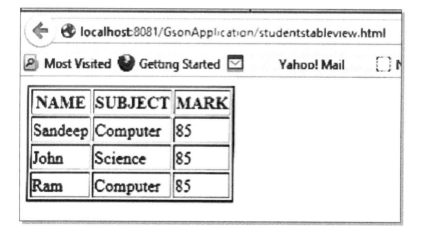

People and places you should get to know

If you need help with GSON, here are some people and places that will prove invaluable:

Official sites

+ Home page: `http://code.google.com/p/google-gson/`
+ Manual and documentation: `http://google-gson.googlecode.com/svn/trunk/gson/docs/javadocs/index.html`
+ Wiki: `http://en.wikipedia.org/wiki/GSON`
+ Source code: `http://code.google.com/p/google-gson/source/checkout`
+ Design document: `https://sites.google.com/site/gson/gson-design-document`
+ Feed: `http://code.google.com/p/google-gson/feeds`

Articles and tutorials

+ User guide from Google: `https://sites.google.com/site/gson/gson-user-guide`
+ Mkyong's blog: `http://www.mkyong.com/java/how-do-convert-java-object-to-from-json-format-gson-api/`

Community

+ Official forums: `https://groups.google.com/forum/?fromgroups#!forum/google-gson`
+ Unofficial forums: `http://stackoverflow.com/questions/tagged/gson`

Blogs

+ Java code geek blog post: `http://examples.javacodegeeks.com/core-java/gson/convert-java-object-to-from-json-using-gson-example/`
+ GSON applications: `http://www.tutorialsavvy.com/search/label/gson`

Thank you for buying
Instant GSON

About Packt Publishing

Packt, pronounced 'packed', published its first book "*Mastering phpMyAdmin for Effective MySQL Management*" in April 2004 and subsequently continued to specialize in publishing highly focused books on specific technologies and solutions.

Our books and publications share the experiences of your fellow IT professionals in adapting and customizing today's systems, applications, and frameworks. Our solution based books give you the knowledge and power to customize the software and technologies you're using to get the job done. Packt books are more specific and less general than the IT books you have seen in the past. Our unique business model allows us to bring you more focused information, giving you more of what you need to know, and less of what you don't.

Packt is a modern, yet unique publishing company, which focuses on producing quality, cutting-edge books for communities of developers, administrators, and newbies alike. For more information, please visit our website: www.packtpub.com.

Writing for Packt

We welcome all inquiries from people who are interested in authoring. Book proposals should be sent to author@packtpub.com. If your book idea is still at an early stage and you would like to discuss it first before writing a formal book proposal, contact us; one of our commissioning editors will get in touch with you.

We're not just looking for published authors; if you have strong technical skills but no writing experience, our experienced editors can help you develop a writing career, or simply get some additional reward for your expertise.

[PACKT]
PUBLISHING

Java Persistence with MyBatis 3

ISBN: 978-1-78216-680-1   Paperback: 132 pages

A practical guide to MyBatis, a simple yet powerful Java Persistence Framework!

1. Detailed instructions on how to use MyBatis with XML and Annotation-based SQL Mappers

2. An in-depth discussion on how to map complex SQL query results such as One-To-Many and Many-To-Many using MyBatis ResultMaps

3. Step-by-step instructions on how to integrate MyBatis with a Spring framework

Apache Tomcat 7 Essentials

ISBN: 978-1-84951-662-4   Paperback: 294 pages

Learn Apache Tomcat 7 step-by-step through a practical approach, achieving a wide vision of enterprise middleware along with building your own middleware servers, and administrating 24x7x365

1. Readymade solution for web technologies for migration/hosting and supporting environment for Tomcat 7

2. Tips, tricks, and best practices for web hosting solution providers for Tomcat 7

3. Content designed with practical approach and plenty of illustrations

Please check **www.PacktPub.com** for information on our titles

jMonkeyEngine 3.0 Beginner's Guide

ISBN: 978-1-84951-646-4   Paperback: 352 pages

Develop professional 3D games for desktop, web, and mobile, all in the familiar Java programming language

1. Create 3D games that run on Android devices, Windows, Mac OS, Linux desktop PCs and in web browsers – for commercial, hobbyists, or educational purposes.

2. Follow end-to-end examples that teach essential concepts and processes of game development, from the basic layout of a scene to interactive game characters.

3. Make your artwork come alive and publish your game to multiple platforms, all from one unified development environment.

HTML5 Game Development with ImpactJS

ISBN: 978-1-84969-456-8   Paperback: 304 pages

A step-by-step guide to developing your own 2D games

1. A practical hands-on approach to teach you how to build your own game from scratch.

2. Learn to incorporate game physics.

3. How to monetize and deploy to the web and mobile platforms.

Please check **www.PacktPub.com** for information on our titles

9 781783 282036